Bigfoot

Therese Shea

The Tony Stead
NONFICTION
INDEPENDENT
READING COLLECTION

Rosen Classroom Books & Materials™
New York.

Published in 2006 by The Rosen Publishing Group, Inc.
29 East 21st Street, New York, NY 10010

Photo credits: Cover, pp. 5, 11, 17, 19 © Bettmann/Corbis; p. 7 © AP Wide World; p. 9 © Werner Forman/Corbis; p. 13 © Corbis; p. 15 © Alexandria Daily Town Talk/AP Wide World; p. 21 © Hulton/Archive.

Library of Congress Cataloging-in-Publication Data

Shea, Therese.
  Bigfoot / Therese Shea.
      p. cm. — (The Tony Stead nonfiction independent reading collection)
  Includes index.
  ISBN 1-4042-5675-X
  1. Sasquatch—Juvenile literature. I. Title. II. Series.
  QL89.2.S2S54 2006
  001.944—dc22

                                                    2005004413

Manufactured in the United States of America

Contents

1 An Unusual Sight   4

2 Who or What Is Bigfoot?   6

3 An Old Tale   8

4 A President's Tale   10

5 Just Stories?   12

6 Kidnapped by Bigfoot   14

7 Caught on Film   16

8 An Explanation   18

9 Where Is Bigfoot?   20

10 Are You a Believer?   22

    Glossary   23

    Index   24

    Web Sites   24

1

An Unusual Sight

Imagine your friend tells you that she has just seen an unusual creature in the forest. It was 9 feet (2.7 m) tall and covered in hair! It was walking like a man and quickly disappeared behind some trees when it saw her. What would you say? Would you believe her? Many people might say that she saw Bigfoot.

This picture shows what Bigfoot may look like,
according to many people's stories.

2

Who or What Is Bigfoot?

In 1958, "Bigfoot" got its name when a bulldozer driver named Jerry Crew found huge footprints in Willow Creek, California. Crew made a **cast** of one of the footprints.

An adult Bigfoot is said to be between 6 feet (1.8 m) and 10 feet (3 m) tall. Its body is covered with thick hair except for parts of its hands, feet, and face. It has a bad smell. It walks upright on two feet, like a human.

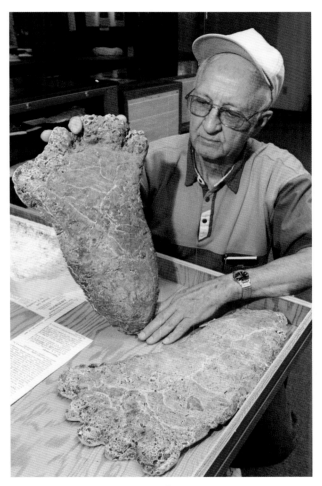

In this photograph, a volunteer at a museum in
Willow Creek, California, holds a plaster cast of a
Bigfoot footprint on display in the museum.

3

An Old Tale

The **legend** of Bigfoot is an old one. Many believe that there are several kinds of creatures like Bigfoot. For many years, Native Americans of western Canada have told stories of giant, hairy creatures that live in the woods. Other names for Bigfoot are Sasquatch, Skookum, and Oh-mah. These are words that are taken from Native American languages.

Some Native American tribes created masks like this one showing the "Wild Man of the Woods." Some wonder if the Wild Man could be a Bigfoot.

4

A President's Tale

A former president of the United States, Theodore Roosevelt, wrote about a Bigfoot in 1892. He told the story of a hunter who found proof of a Bigfoot near his camp in Idaho. The hunter saw the big footprints of a creature that walked on two feet. Unlike a bear, this creature had toes and no claws. Most stories about Bigfoot describe a peaceful creature.

This picture shows Phil Thompson, a hunter who discovered a Bigfoot print near Coos Bay, Oregon, in 1976. The footprint measured 17 inches (43.2 cm) long.

5

Just Stories?

If there is one Bigfoot or more out there, why doesn't anyone have proof? Several people claim to have caught a Bigfoot at some time. In 1884, a newspaper in British Columbia, Canada, reported the capture of a small creature that matched the description of Bigfoot in every way but size. Some think that the story was just a **hoax**. Others think the creature was actually a **chimpanzee** that a sailor had brought back from Africa.

Forests would be good hiding places for a Bigfoot. Many forests have not been fully explored.

6

Kidnapped by Bigfoot

Albert Ostman, a lumberjack, claimed that a Bigfoot picked him up while he was sleeping in a forest in British Columbia. He said the Bigfoot carried him to its family. Ostman said he stayed with the Bigfoot and its family for about a week before he escaped. Although Ostman said that he was taken in 1924, he did not tell anyone his story until 1957. He thought no one would believe him.

Do you think that this footprint really belongs to Bigfoot, or is it a fake?

7

Caught on Film

A famous piece of proof of Bigfoot was presented in 1967. Roger Patterson and Robert Gimlin filmed what they said was Bigfoot in Bluff Creek Valley, California. The creature on film is either a real Bigfoot or a person in a **costume**. Over the years, other films and footprints have been proven to be false. No one has ever been able to prove that this film of Bigfoot is fake.

Different footprints were found in the same area where this creature was filmed. Some people think that more than one Bigfoot lived around this area.

8

An Explanation

Some scientists think Bigfoot may be related to humans the same way humans are related to **primates** like gorillas. Perhaps a **species** of primate that we thought had died out, such as the "Giant Ape," is still alive. Based on the **fossils** of the Giant Ape that have been found, some scientists think this primate was about 9 feet (2.7 m) tall, walked on two legs, and was covered with hair.

This photograph, taken in 1974, shows the late Dr. Grover Krantz holding casts of footprints he thought were made by a Bigfoot in southwestern Washington.

9

Where Is Bigfoot?

Most Bigfoot sightings have taken place in the forests of the northwestern United States and western Canada. However, according to the Bigfoot Field Researchers Organization, there have been sightings all over North America. There have also been reports of a similar creature in the Himalaya mountains of southern Asia. This creature, called a Yeti, is also known as the Abominable Snowman because it lives in an area that is always snowy.

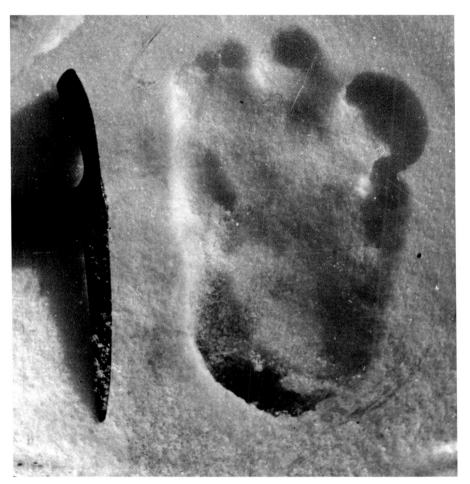

Many people believe the Yeti left footprints in the
mountains, which are proof that it had been there.
Other people believe that the Yeti does not exist.

10

Are You a Believer?

Perhaps you still need more proof of Bigfoot. Maybe you think someone should have captured one by now. Scientists once thought that other creatures did not exist—like the African mountain gorilla, the **Komodo dragon**, and the giant panda. We now know they exist. One thing is for certain: If a Bigfoot does exist, it is shy. Maybe it does not want to be found!

Glossary

cast (KAST) A model made of an object or footprint.

chimpanzee (chim-PAN-zee) An African ape that lives mostly in the trees.

costume (KAHS-toom) An outfit worn to make someone look like something else.

fossil (FAH-suhl) The hardened remains of a dead animal or plant that lived long ago.

hoax (HOHKS) A trick.

Komodo dragon (kuh-MOH-doh DRA-guhn) The largest of all lizards on Earth.

legend (LEH-juhnd) A story that has been told for many years that may or may not be true.

primate (PRY-mayt) A member of a group of animals that includes monkeys, chimpanzees, and humans.

species (SPEE-sheez) A group of animals that share the same basic features.

Index

A
Abominable Snowman, 20
Asia, 20

B
Bigfoot Field Researchers Organization, 20
British Columbia, Canada, 12, 14

C
California, 6, 16
Canada, 8, 20
cast, 6
Crew, Jerry, 6

F
film(s), 16
footprints, 6, 10, 16

G
Gimlin, Robert, 16

H
hair(y), 4, 6, 8, 18
Himalaya mountains, 20

I
Idaho, 10

N
Native American(s), 8
North America, 20

O
Oh-mah, 8
Ostman, Albert, 14

P
Patterson, Roger, 16
primate(s), 18

R
Roosevelt, Theodore, 10

S
Sasquatch, 8
Skookum, 8

U
United States, 10, 20

Y
Yeti, 20

Web Sites

Due to the changing nature of Internet links, the Rosen Publishing Group, Inc., has developed an online list of Web sites related to the subject of this book. This site is updated regularly. Please use this link to access the list:
http://www.rcbmlinks.com/tsirc/bigfoot/